little book BIG idea

What is history?

Noodle JUICE

Noodle Juice Ltd
www.noodle-juice.com
Stonesfield House, Stanwell Lane, Great Bourton, Oxfordshire, OX17 1QS
First published in Great Britain 2023

Text by Noodle Juice 2023 • Illustrations by Katie Rewse 2023

Printed in China
A CIP catalogue record of this book is available from the British Library.
ISBN: 978-1-915613-72-1
1 3 5 7 9 10 8 6 4 2

FSC
www.fsc.org
MIX
Paper | Supporting responsible forestry
FSC® C005748

This book is made from FSC®-certified paper. By choosing this book, you help to take care of the world's forests. Learn more: www.fsc.org.

What is history?

History is the study of the past. It's the study of people, of decisions made or not, of actions taken or not and how they affected the way we live our lives.

Let's ask some questions to see if we can work out what history means to us!

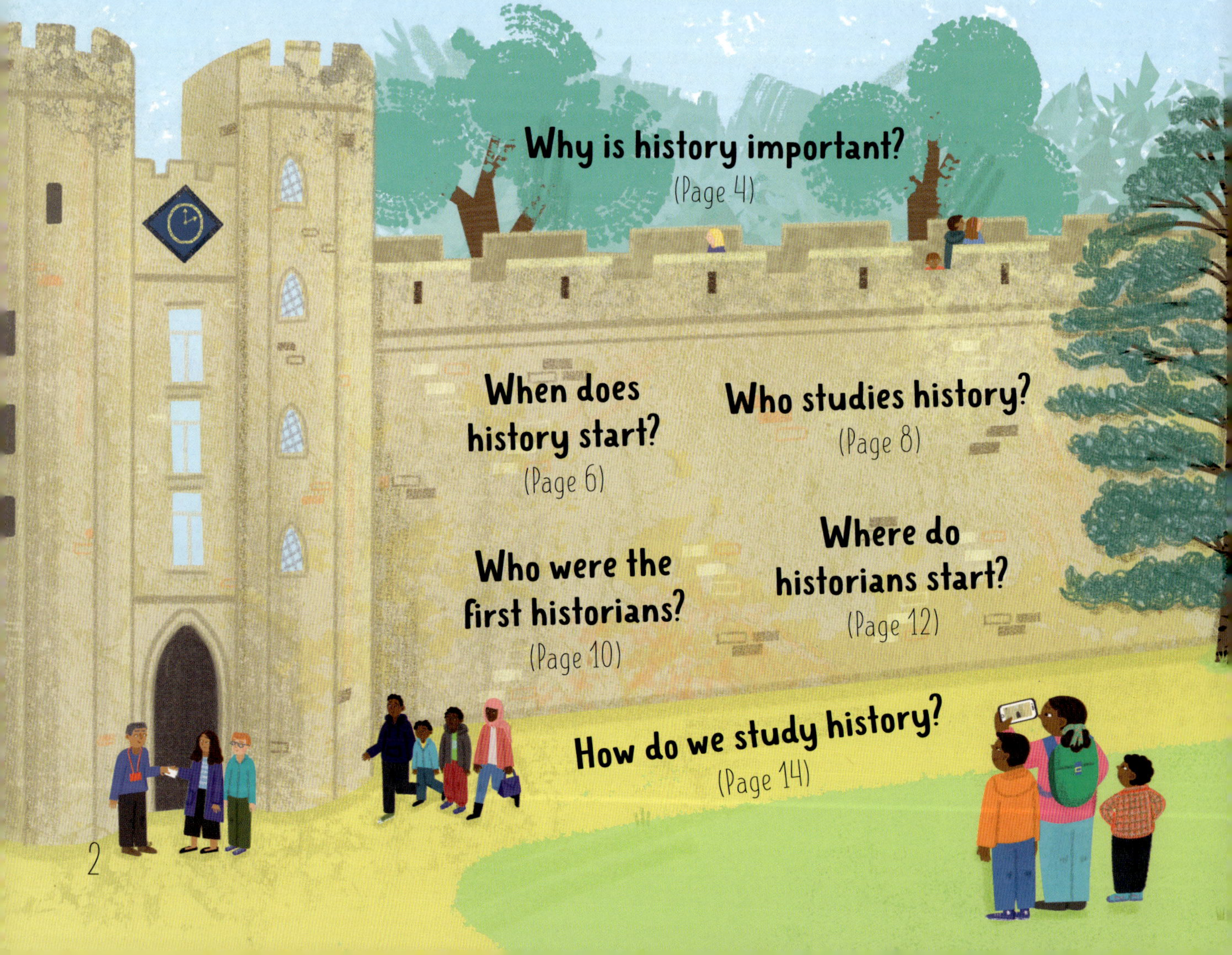

Are there different types of history?
(Page 16)

What are the different ages of history?
(Page 18)

Who was important in the past?
(Page 20)

Whose stories haven't been told?
(Page 22)

Who should we believe?
(Page 24)

How can history help people?
(Page 26)

Why is history important?

History is important because it helps us to understand WHY things happen. If we understand why something good happens, we can try to repeat it. If we understand why something bad happens, we must try to not make the same mistake again.

History can help us to discover how people **lived** in the past.

Studying history can help us to learn from our mistakes and make better **decisions**.

It allows us to explore different cultures and see how they **change** over time.

History can also teach us how to be **better** human beings.

When does history start?

History begins when people started to keep written records. The earliest forms of writing we have discovered are almost 5,000 years old. Ancient Egyptians used pictures called hieroglyphs. Say it like this:

HI-RO-glifs

to record information about the pharoahs, the leaders of their people.

At the same time, the Sumerians, who lived in the area that is now Iraq, developed a different writing system called cuneiform. In China, ideograms or symbols were used to record lists of its rulers.

Two thousand years later, ancient Greeks and ancient Romans wrote accounts that studied **why** things happened.

The Middle Ages (1000 CE–1300 CE) provided many written sources for historians to study.

During the 17th and 18th centuries, people began to write histories of their nations focusing on **great achievements** or leaders.

By the 20th century, it became important to study how the **whole** of society lived, not just the famous, influential or wealthy.

* CE stands for Common Era which started at the year 0000. BCE stands for Before Common Era. This book was published in 2023 CE.

Who studies history?

If you study history, you are called a 'historian'. History is huge. It covers over 5,000 years, as well as the whole planet, so most historians choose a part of history to study.

Some historians choose a specific period. They might concentrate on a particular **century**, decade or year.

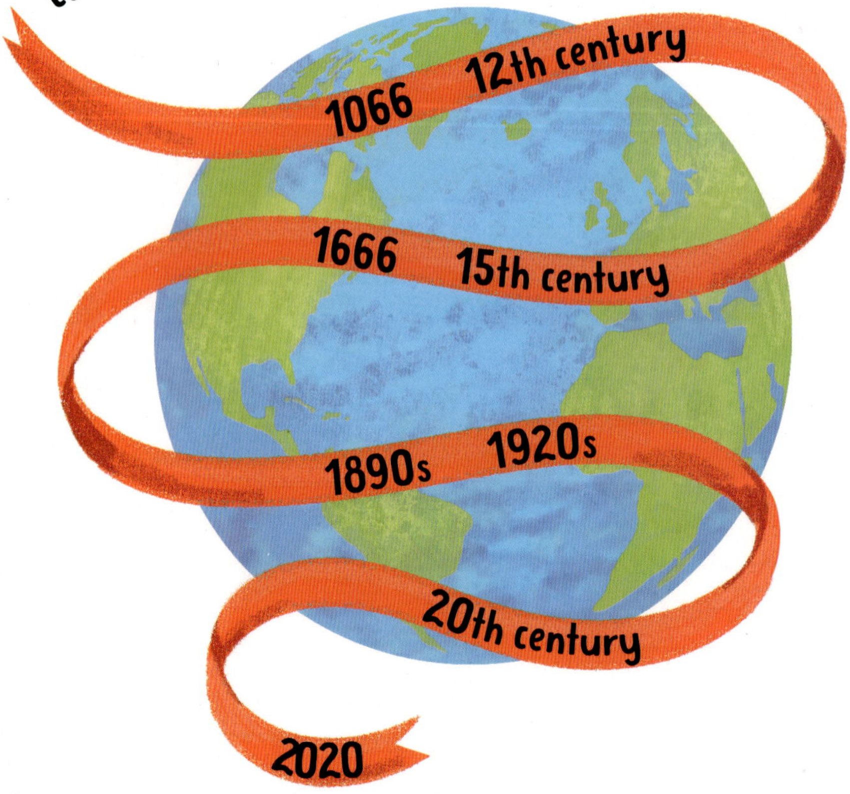

Others might choose a single **country** or geographical area.

Historians can also choose to study a specific subject, such as...

Fashion

Transport

Battles

Exploration

Technology

Politics

Kings and queens

Music

Art

Which subject would you like to study?

Who were the first historians?

The famous Chinese philosopher, **Confucius**, is believed to have written a text called 'Classic of History'.

The Father of History, **Herodotus**, wrote an account of the Greco-Persian wars.

Thucydides, an ancient Greek, wrote about the Peloponnesian War.

Sima Qian studied Chinese history up to the creation of the Han Dynastry in 206 BCE.

During the height of the Roman Empire, three historians stood out as recorders of what happened.

Polybius was actually Greek, but was the first to write a history of Rome's success.

Tacitus wrote the first biography of the Roman emperors, Tiberius, Claudius and Nero.

Livy recorded the transformation of Rome from a republic into an empire.

Where do historians start?

There are lots of different places that historians can look to find out information about the past. Historians call these 'sources' and they can be split into two different types.

Primary sources are first-hand accounts about events or time periods from people who were there when it happened.

Official records

Photographs

Ancient ruins

Diaries

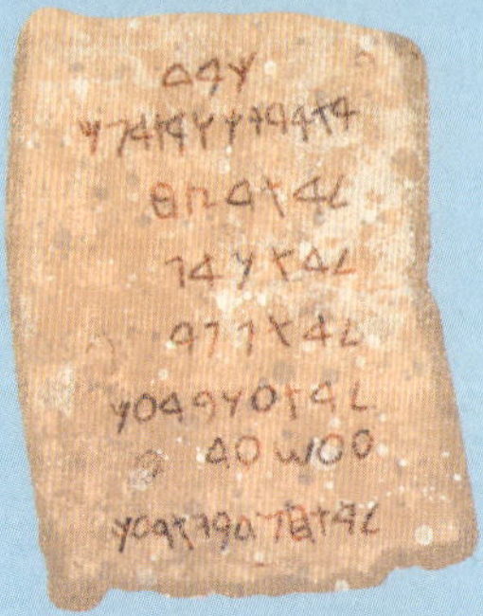

Stone tablets

Letters

Paintings

Sculptures

Television documentaries

Reviews

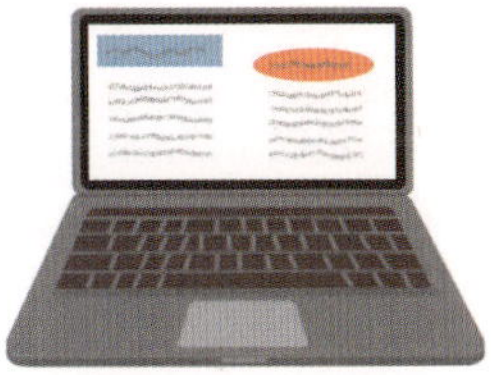

Newspapers

Books

Secondary sources are extra information that help us to understand the first-hand accounts.

A historian who studies the past through physical objects is called an 'archaeologist'. Say it like this:

ARK-ee-ol-oh-GIST

They carefully dig up and uncover things that give us clues about how people used to live.

How do we study history?

The best way to study history is to ask questions.

Then you need to find proof for those answers. For example, here's a picture of someone from the early 20th century. What questions might you ask about it?

What is the man wearing?

What does that tell us about him?

What job does the woman do?

Where do you think they both might be?

Remember, it's always good to have more than one source for your answer.

What are the different ages of history?

Time has been divided into different periods, called 'ages' or 'eras'. They can then be divided further. Often in British history, a period might be named after the kings or queens of the time, such as Georgian or Victorian.

The Stone Age

3.3 million to 3,000 years ago

It was so-called because humans used stones as tools or weapons.

The Bronze Age

3,000 BCE to 1,200 BCE

Humans discovered how to make bronze tools by melting copper and tin together.

The Iron Age

1,200 BCE to 510 BCE

Iron weapons and tools were harder than bronze so gave people an advantage in battle.

The Classical Era

510 BCE to 476 CE

The time of the ancient Greek and ancient Roman empires.

The Medieval Era

476 BCE to 1,450 CE

This period of almost 1,000 years saw the Crusades, the Black Plague and the invention of the printing press.

The Early Modern Era

1,450 CE to 1,750 CE

The time of the Renaissance, where artists, composers, writers, scientists and explorers took centre stage.

The Modern Era

1,750 CE to present

Wars and industrial expansion, as well as revolutions in America, France and Greece, saw a boom in population as well as technology.

Are there different types of history?

There are many different types of history that historians can choose to study. Here are six of the main categories.

Political history explores how **governments** rule. It looks at the different political parties, and events and movements.

Diplomatic history considers how different **international countries or states** work together or against each other.

Social history studies how **different groups** in society behave. It looks at families, crime, poverty, health and how people earn money.

Cultural history includes the history of **art, music and literature**, as well as studying the way people live together in groups.

Intellectual history studies the history of **ideas** and human thinking.

Economic history studies the history of **money** and finance, as well as how a country's economy performs.

People can also choose to study the history of a geographical region.

Who was important in the past?

The people who were considered important were those who had an impact on society or their country. Historians wrote about rulers, generals, politicians and leaders of countries.

Wealthy individuals were also singled out because their wealth allowed them to have an effect on society, either by employing people, sponsoring artists or simply influencing those in power.

In the past, history was often written by the victors or **winners** of battles or wars.

This means that we don't always know the full story. In fact, some stories are MISSING altogether.

Whose stories haven't been told?

In the past, there were groups of people whose voices weren't heard. These groups may have been oppressed, ignored or considered less important by the ruling classes of the time.

Not that long ago, your **gender** played a part in whether you were included in history. Most women were excluded as their role in society didn't play a part in the history of the time.

Your **race** could also mean that your voice wasn't heard.

Who you **love** meant that sometimes you weren't included.

If you were **poor**, you were unlikely to be mentioned in history books.

This all started to change during the twentieth century, and now historians study everyone's history.

Who should we believe?

Most history has been written by men, which means, as we've already noticed, that a woman's perspective is probably missing. But we also need to think about something called 'bias'.

Bias is when the way we think about things is AFFECTED by our experiences or what we believe. Our perception or point of view might not be totally accurate. If we aren't aware of our own biases, we can become prejudiced.

If you see a classmate with torn and dirty clothes, you might think they are **poor**...

but they could have had an accident, or spilled their lunch.

If someone you **like** says something horrible, you might excuse them because they could be having a bad day...

but if someone you **don't like** says the same thing, you might see that as another reason to dislike them.

If many people have similar biases, that can affect how a society **treats** people.

You can choose to believe who you want, but it's always sensible to know or try to work out what biases that person may have.

How can history help people?

History changes. Every day we may learn something new about the past. Understanding our past can help us improve our future.

Understanding different nations and cultures helps us speak to others with **respect**.

Learning how to study history means you can **analyse and interpret** information quickly.

We can be inspired by **brilliant** people from the past,

Learning to **connect** events, so we know how something started, means we might work out how things end.

We should also be able to **learn** from our mistakes.

People often want to study their personal history and may find **family** they didn't realise they had.

Understanding history can help us all.

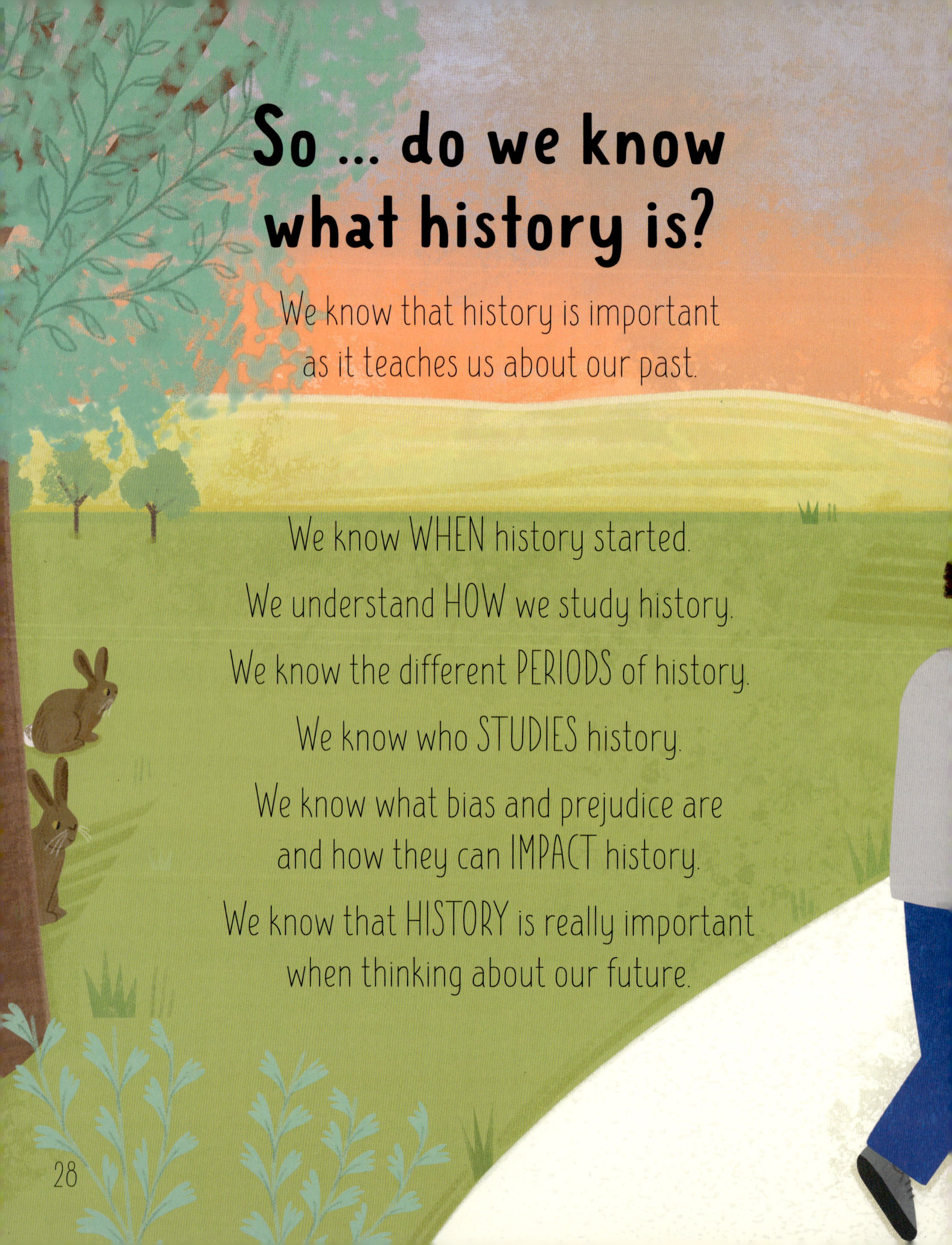

So ... do we know what history is?

We know that history is important as it teaches us about our past.

We know WHEN history started.

We understand HOW we study history.

We know the different PERIODS of history.

We know who STUDIES history.

We know what bias and prejudice are and how they can IMPACT history.

We know that HISTORY is really important when thinking about our future.

But history is speeding up. More and more information is available to us every day. We need to understand which bits are IMPORTANT and which parts we can IGNORE.

Why don't you think about your history and what you would like your future to be?

Glossary

Account a report or description of an event or experience

Achievement a thing done well, with effort

Advantage something that puts one in a favourable position

Ages a distinct period of history

Analyse examine something carefully and in detail

Archeologist someone who studies the past through physical objects

Battle a fight between large, organised armed forces

Biography an account of someone's life written by someone else

Black Plague a 14th century European pandemic

Century a period of one hundred years

Crusades European military expeditions to the Holy Land during the Middle Ages

Culture humans' intellectual and artistic achievements

Decade a period of ten years

Economics concerned with the making of, use of and transfer of wealth

Empire a group of countries ruled by one leader

Era a long and distinct period of history

Expansion becoming larger or more extensive

Finance the management of large amounts of money

General a commander of an army

Ideograms a symbol for a thing that doesn't include the sounds used to say it

Industrial to do with industry

Interpret to explain the meaning of something

Leader a person who commands a group or country

Oppressed subject to harsh and unjust treatment

Period a length of portion of time

Pharoah a ruler in ancient Egypt

Politician a person who works in government

Prejudice a biased opinion not based in fact or experience

Printing press a machine for printing words or pictures from plates

Proof evidence to establish a fact or the truth in a statement

Record evidence about the past, especially a written account

Renaissance a period in European history when art and literature thrived

Republic a state ruled by someone elected by the people

Respect appreciation for someone or something

Ruler a person who is in charge of a country or state

Social concerned with society

Society a group of people who live together in an ordered community

Sponsor someone who supports and pays the costs for someone else, often artistic

Sumerian someone who lived in ancient Babylon

Technology using science to solve problems

Transformation a marked change in appearance or form

Tudor the period in English history between 1485 and 1603

Victorian the period Queen Victoria was on the English throne

Victor the person who defeats their opponent in battle or competition